Five I.D.E.A.L. Strategies to Achieve Financial Freedom

Five I.D.E.A.L. Strategies to Achieve Financial Freedom

BREAK THE CHAINS OF FINANCIAL SLAVERY FOREVER

Yveline L. Dalmacy

ISBN-13: 9781534761018
ISBN-10: 1534761012
Library of Congress Control Number: 2016911687
CreateSpace Independent Publishing Platform
North Charleston, South Carolina

Table of Contents

Preface

Congratulations! Thank you for buying this book. There is no doubt that you are looking to make a change in your personal finances.

The five I.D.E.A.L. strategies contained will hopefully, as of today, put you on the path to financial wellness. Upon reading this book, you will be armed with five different strategies to improve your financial well-being. Did you know that according to the US Bureau of the Census, median household income as of 2014 was only $53,482 and per capita income in the preceding twelve months (in 2014 dollars) was only $28,555? The percentage of the US population that was in poverty in 2014 was 14.8. To reiterate, in 2014, 14.8 percent of the US population lived in poverty; a majority of people are one paycheck away from poverty. Don't be a statistic—secure your financial future today!

It is a fact that most single men and women do not have any retirement savings. This book can serve as your road map to a more fulfilled financial future; it will teach you basic matters related to credit and finance by using the five I.D.E.A.L. strategies outlined.

It is my greatest wish that you find yourself on a more sustainable path to financial freedom after reading this book.

Five I.D.E.A.L. Strategies to Achieve Financial Freedom was written with young adults in mind to give them a general overview of personal financial-management strategies. This book is not meant to replace the advice of a qualified certified public accountant, financial planner, or any similar professional. The material provided in this book should be deemed reliable; however, part of this book may be affected by changes in the law or by interpretations of the law since the book was written.

About the Author

Yveline L. Dalmacy has a master's in business administration with a specialization in banking and finance. She has over twenty years of experience working in the banking and financial industry. She also holds a master's in diplomacy and international relations with specializations in international economics and development and global health and human security.

She interned at the Department of Commerce as a White House liaison in SelectUSA. She considers herself privileged to have had that opportunity.

With the experience that she has gained from her work and her education, Mrs. Dalmacy gives back to her community by teaching people about credit, savings, and budgeting on a community radio show that she hosts with Dr. Kesler Dalmacy.

Mrs. Dalmacy is passionate about helping others, and her greatest wish is to be able to help people reach their next-highest financial level. She is also passionate about world politics—she keeps abreast of national and international news on a daily basis.

Mrs. Dalmacy is a trained entrepreneur and real-estate investor. She believes in the Kaizen philosophy and lives a life of continuous growth and perfection. She is an avid reader of all sort of books who firmly believes in education and its power to change lives for the better.

You may contact Mrs. Yveline Dalmacy at Info@IDEAL.COM.

Acknowledgments

All praise and thanks to God for blessing me and my family and for giving me guidance, vision, and the courage to embark on writing this book and see it come to fruition.

I would like to thank my mother, Marie Ford, for her love and for being my inspiration and role model; my grandmother for instilling in me a philanthropic spirit; and my husband, Doctor Kesler Dalmacy, for being the wind beneath my wings and for his love and his support in helping me follow my dreams. I would also like to thank my beautiful daughters, Tatiana and Anabelle; my brothers, Yves and Kris; my loving sister, Ludnie Joubert; her husband; and all my beautiful nieces.

In addition, my thanks goes out to my aunt and cousins; the Dioro family in Haiti, superheroes in my eyes for being professionals in their own right despite countless adversities; my former boss, Atara Aharonovitz; my broker, Arlene Trunzo; and my alma mater, Seton Hall University. I send a world of thanks to my professors: Dr. Catherine Ruby, Dr. Assefaw Bariagaber, Dr. Martin Edwards, Dr. Li-Wen Zhang (my role model), Dr. Edislav Manetovic, Dr. Ann Marie Murphy, and Dr. Aaron Hale. I also thank my great friends: Beverley Brown; Michelle Cooper; Danielle Gabriel; Ednise Jean-Baptist; Dionne L. Jordan, Wilner Altidort; Serge Rodriguez and his daughter, Nadiah; my inspiration, Carole Y. Picard; and my in-laws, the Dalmacy, Tardieu, and Francois families. Thanks also go to my friends in Georgia: Dr. Tracey Wallace, Mrs. Lisa Hall, Kikine, Sharon Arrieta, and Anthony Fernandez.

To my colleagues and managers at the US Department of Commerce, thank you for having accepted me, an immigrant, to be a White House liaison intern in the spring of 2012. It was an incredible experience, one I cherish to this day.

INTRODUCTION

I.D.E.A.L. Financial Freedom: Break the Chains of Financial Slavery with Five Easy Strategies

D o you want to stop being a slave to your debt? Do you wish to do something to increase your savings? Do you want to stop struggling to make ends meet? At some point in our lives, we have all asked ourselves these questions or similar ones. But the most important questions we need to ask ourselves have yet to be asked. Are you willing to look at your financial situation through a microscope? Are you willing to do the work that is required to free yourself from your financial burden? If your answer to each is yes, know that you are not alone. Your past financial habits should not determine your future. You can achieve financial freedom, but are you willing to do the work necessary to achieve the freedom that you crave?

First, you must believe that it is possible to achieve financial freedom and stop being a slave to your debt. Whatever is holding you back is keeping you enslaved to your finances; know that you now have the tools to dissect your debts, to trim them to a more manageable level in order to have a better financial future.

It used to be that to become financially independent you got a good education, got a good job after you graduated, worked twenty or twenty-five years, and by the time you retired, you were financially well-off from money invested in your 401(k) plan, the pension you got from the company you worked for, your savings, and Social Security. Today's reality is much different. You sacrifice so much to go to school for a good education and hope that by the time you graduate you can get a job. Otherwise, you end up working a job that offers you minimum wage while you wait for your boat to pull in. First, not many companies offer a pension plan or a matching 401(k), for that matter. Basically, we are on our own. It is up to us to find our own golden parachute by any means necessary. To embark on the journey to financial independence, you need tools, a plan, and a commitment to stick to that plan. This book will lay out five easy strategies that can help you and your children get on the road to financial success or, at the very least, have a more clear idea about your personal finance and what you will need to achieve your financial goal, whether your goal is to own a home, buy a car, save for your children's college education, or save for retirement. I promise you that you will find something worthwhile in this book that will help you free yourself from financial slavery with the five I.D.E.A.L. strategies that I will explain in further detail in the next chapters.

I am using the term "financial enslavement" in this book to make a point. What I mean is that if you work and don't have enough to pay your bills and live a sufficiently financially stress-free life, then your finances are enslaved! If your monthly debt exceeds your net monthly income, you are financially enslaved. I used to be in a similar situation. Right after my divorce from my first husband, we were still friendly and wanted to amicably resolve our problems. We agreed to be responsible for the credit-card debts we had individually initiated, though we were jointly responsible for the debt. Wanting to be a good ex-wife, I agreed wholeheartedly. Because we never had problems paying our credit-cards bills, I was thinking of our joint income and didn't realize that once my ex-husband was gone, my income would be insufficient to pay our joint debts.

Within months of our separation, I found myself financially enslaved from head to toe. I was not making enough to pay the maintenance on my co-op, phone bill, cable bill, or numerous credit-card bills and student loans. Once I signed the divorce papers, even the small amount of child support was not coming in regularly. Basically, I was in a financial mess. I kept descending further into debt and had to use my credit cards to supplement my income. Although I was a college graduate at the time, the money I was making couldn't meet my financial obligations.

A friend of mine suggested that I declare bankruptcy and, not having a choice at the time, I did. I was not as financially literate then as I am now, so I followed my friend's advice and declared bankruptcy. In my culture, it is a great shame to have to declare bankruptcy. We pride ourselves on being self-sufficient, paying our bills on time, and not having to depend on a government subsidy—even if we are starving! Imagine my shame, as a college graduate, to find myself in bankruptcy court. It is a shame that I carry to this day, but I vowed to learn as much as possible about finance and help others that have been or are or in a similar situation.

To have financial freedom, you should be able to live fairly well, be able to pay your bills on time, have enough to put food on the table, not have to depend on the government for help, and be able to save a portion of your income for retirement. If you cannot do most of these things, if not all, then you are financially enslaved.

You are financially enslaved when you work two jobs and still struggle to pay the bills, debt collectors are calling you at work, you cannot afford to buy your child a present for the holidays, or your spouse looks at you with disappointment in his or her eyes. You know you are in trouble when the bills are mounting and you are a hardworking individual, yet you struggle to make ends meet. The opposite could also be true: you work hard and are able to purchase your dream house, you live comfortably, you are one of the few who are able to put food on the table, and you are able to travel at least once a year. If you happen to own your house free and clear, congratulations! You may not be financially enslaved. A house is one of the biggest investments in your lifetime. Having a place to call your own is a big achievement, but if you owe a mortgage on your house, you are not as financially free as you think. Some people would tell you that it is good to owe a mortgage for the tax deduction that it offers, but wouldn't you rather own your home free and clear? That, in my opinion, would be a great accomplishment, to say, "I own this house free and clear. No one can take it away from me, unless I don't pay the taxes, water, and sewer on the property."

Debt and your credit score have an inverse relationship. The higher your debt relative to your income, the lower your credit score. Saving and investing have a positive relationship: the more you save, the more you have to invest in your financial future.

Free yourself from financial slavery with these five I.D.E.A.L. strategies to achieve financial freedom:

Increase your credit score and credit limit.
Decrease high-interest debt.
Establish a budget.
Accumulate wealth through savings and investments.
Live below your means.

For these I.D.E.A.L. strategies to work, the first thing you need to ask yourself is what financial freedom feels like. Each of us has his or her own interpretation of what it means to be financially free. At what level of wealth would it feel that you have made it and have achieved your goal? Are you at a point where your inner voice tells you that you still have work to do, or do you feel confident that you have enough money to weather whatever storm life may throw at you? Once you are in that position, rest assured that you are financially free.

If you want to achieve financial freedom, you have to cultivate an inner feeling of financial abundance. You have to consider yourself financially free while you are working toward your goal of achieving financial freedom. So give yourself a time frame—calculate how long it will take you to achieve your goals of achieving financial freedom and what it will take to get you there. Wanting to be financially free is one thing; working toward that goal to make it happen is another. Do not procrastinate on putting plans in place to achieve financial freedom. Generally speaking, you are more likely to find thorns on your path than roses or gold. What matters is that you stay the course and never give up. One day soon, you will have achieved your goal. That goes for almost everything in life. If you want something badly enough, you have to be willing to make the sacrifices it requires to achieve your end goal. Once you are determined to see your goal through, you will be amazed at how much support you receive from the universe, family, and friends. As with almost everything in life, persistence and determination are key. You will find that once you put some action behind your goals, you are more than likely to achieve them. As the saying goes, "Always reach for the stars, and if you don't reach the stars, you will have landed among the clouds." If you are determined to achieve your financial freedom, you must put some action behind the intention. As you embark on your journey to financial freedom, stay positive, stay the course, and you will find that in due time you will have achieved your goal. But first, you have to take the initial step toward fulfilling your goal and ambition.

Stay committed to reading this book; you will find that there is at least one thing you can do to positively affect your finances. The ideas proposed have the potential to get you to a higher financial level; at a minimum, the potential exists to get you credit wise. So don't be afraid to start putting your financial house in order; follow some of the strategies, if not all of them, to get you at least on the road to a more secure financial future. Remember not to feel ashamed or guilty about the financial position that you are in. What you should feel ashamed about is not doing anything to improve your financial situation. Again, the idea is not to judge or be critical—that is not my intent. My intention is to put the thought in your head, the belief that a better financial circumstance awaits you, but you have to take that first step; you have to want to help yourself succeed financially. Now, let us focus on arming you with the tools, techniques, and strategies that you need to make yourself financially free, or at least to bring you closer to achieving the dream of financial freedom.

You have already made the first step toward securing a better financial future by buying a copy of this book. I suggest that you share the knowledge contained with your friends and family; more specifically, with your college- or school-aged children. Our children need to start making the right financial decisions for themselves now;

they need to be equipped with the specific knowledge that they can do better than their elders. Having our children achieving their dreams of being financially independent must be one of the greatest rewards parents can experience. Use this book to get your children to start forming great habits regarding finance and hopefully they will be better prepared to handle the ups and downs inherent in their future financial lives.

CHAPTER 1

Increase Your Credit Limit and Credit Score

First, let's define a credit score. A credit score tells your financial story. It tells banks, credit-card companies, businesses, and other credit companies how likely you are to repay your debt when you borrow money. It really is that simple. Credit scores range from 300 to 850—the higher your score, the better. A higher score makes it easier for you to qualify for loans and credit cards.

One thing I have learned about credit is that it can make or break you. With bad credit, everything—the car you buy, the house you mortgage, or the student loans you take out—becomes more expensive.

You may wonder what goes into a credit score. Your credit score is based on information in your credit report or credit history. Once you apply for credit from a creditor, how you pay back your loan gets reported by your creditors to the credit-reporting agencies. As of the writing of this book, there are three major credit-reporting agencies: Equifax, Trans Union, and Experian.

Factors that affect your credit score vary widely. You have to understand those factors in order to improve your credit score. The factors that affect your score range from the number of credit accounts you have open—gasoline cards, store cards, credit cards, and others—to the length of time you have held these accounts. The longer you have credit—good credit, that is—the more positively it affects your credit score.

How close you are to your credit limit can also impact your credit score. Another factor that affects your credit is how often your payments have been late. The number of accounts you have in collection can also have a negative impact on your credit score. Collections are unwise if you want to maintain a high credit score. Avoid collections at any cost! If you are unable to make the minimum payment amount that is due on your credit account, call your creditors and make another payment arrangement with them because often they can be very flexible. Whatever you do, do not let any of your accounts be sent to collection.

To raise your credit score, you must pay your bills before their due date or, at the latest, by the due date. Something that can help you stay current on paying your bills is to set up automatic recurring payments. That way, you will not miss making a payment for the month. Just be sure you have enough money in your account to cover the recurring payments you have set up. You don't want to be hit with overdraft and other fees!

Do not get too close to your credit limit. Experts recommend that you do not go above 30 percent of your total credit limit. For example, if your limit is $1,000 on a credit card, at no point should you owe more than $300, which is the equivalent of 30 percent of your credit limit.

It is essential that you check your credit reports regularly. If you have accounts that have been closed, make sure they are not reported as open accounts on your credit report. By checking your credit report at least once every three months, you are likely to catch any reporting errors made by the reporting agencies.

You certainly do not want a closed account to show as being open on your credit report and reflecting a balance that you have actually paid off. Checking your report ensures that you catch these errors on time. You also have to make sure that any account you have open does not appear more than once on your account. This would tend to lower your credit score, since your report would show that you owe more than you actually do.

You also do not want to close any accounts that you have had for a long time. The longer you hold a credit account open, the better it is for your credit score. Last but not least, apply for additional credit only if you need to. Do not be taken in by banks' low-interest-rate credit-card offers. The low-interest rate more often than not applies to balance transfers to the card; any purchases you make using the card will assess a regular interest rate. Check the fine print before you accept any of these offers.

By checking your credit report regularly, you can react quickly to credit reporting that is detrimental to your credit score. These mistakes have a tendency to lower your credit score; the sooner you catch them and are able to get them reversed, the better for your score.

By law, you are entitled to obtain one free copy of your credit report from each of the three credit-reporting agencies. You may get a copy of your credit report at www. annualcreditreport.com or by calling (877) 322-8228. Your report should come with instructions regarding how to dispute an error on your credit.

Once you get your free copy of your credit report, check it thoroughly to ensure that your name, address, and phone number is reported correctly. Make sure you look for credit accounts that do not belong to you or late payments that may have been reported incorrectly.

Once you notice that an error has been made on your credit report, do not waste any time getting it corrected. Remember that negative errors lower your credit score, which makes anything you purchase on credit more expensive.

To fix a credit-reporting mistake, you should first call your creditor to advise him or her that an error has been made on your credit report. Then, call the credit bureau that is reporting the incorrect information and advise it of the error. Be sure to explain fully to the credit-reporting agency the inaccuracy.

Within thirty days, you should hear back from the reporting credit agency. It should stipulate whether the inaccurate item has been removed from your credit file; if it has not been removed, the agency should be able to tell you why they believe the information to be accurate. In any event, they should provide you with a new copy of your credit report that should be updated with the incorrect item removed, which will likely result in an increase of your credit score.

If you believe the information to be inaccurate and the credit-reporting agency refuses to remove the incorrect information, you have recourse by filing a complaint with the Consumer Financial Protection Bureau:

Consumer Financial Protection Bureau
PO Box 4503
Iowa City, Iowa 52244

CHAPTER 2

Decrease High-Interest Debts

Should you ever be in the position where a debt collector has to call you to demand payment, be sure to get the name of the debt collector; the debt collection company's name, address, and phone number; the creditor in question; the amount you owe; and attempt to verify that the debt is in fact yours. Collect this information during the first conversation you have with the debt collector and be sure to get the information in writing prior to starting any negotiation to repay the debt.

It is in your best interest to know your state's statute of limitations for filing a lawsuit to collect the debt. That debt may not be recoverable if it has exceeded your state's statute of limitations. Before you do anything, verify that the debt is actually yours. If the debt is not yours, write the debt collector and tell him or her that the debt isn't yours and that he or she should not contact you again.

Many experts agree that if you want to eliminate debt you must start with the highest interest-rate account first. If you pay monthly, bi-monthly, or quarterly, try to pay as much as possible. Simultaneously, continue to pay at least the minimum payment due on your other debts. In other words, you must continue to meet your other debt obligations while you pay more than the minimum on the highest interest-rate debt in question.

Experts recommend that once you have paid off the debt with the highest interest rate, take the payment amount that you were contributing toward that particular debt and add it to the minimum amount you are making toward the next-highest interest-rate debt account. Once that debt is paid off, use the same strategy to eliminate your next-highest interest-rate debt and so forth. After you are free from your debt or after you have significantly reduced your debt obligations, you may have access to more of your cash flow and it would be wise to start setting money aside for an emergency.

The minimum-recommended amount by most experts is at least three to six months of income. If you can allocate more, even better. It is estimated that if you were to lose your job, it would take a minimum of three to six months to secure another. Your emergency fund is a cushion to assist you in your time of need. We hope that you never have to deal with an emergency situation, but the possibility exists that you may be hit with job loss or an illness, whether yours or a parent's or child's.

Another strategy recommended by a majority of experts is to pay yourself first. Some experts also recommend paying off the smallest debt first and using that win or victory to propel yourself onward and give you the momentum to stay on track.

Table 1. Distribution of Debt, By Net Worth Quintiles and Selected Characteristics: 2011

Characteristic	Number of Households (in thousands)	Net Worth Quintiles									
		Lowest Quintile		Second Quintile		Third Quintile		Fourth Quintile		Highest Quintile	
		Median Debt	Mean Debt	Median Debt	Mean Debt	Median Debt	Mean Debt	Median Debt	Mean Debt	Median Debt	Mean Debt
HOUSEHOLDS											
Total	118,689	17,500	90,228	700	33,043	35,500	78,381	30,900	95,089	41,000	140,704
Race and Hispanic Origin of Householder											
White alone	96,072	15,000	92,098	5,000	48,814	36,000	80,014	30,000	97,125	40,000	139,774
White alone, not Hispanic	83,245	14,000	88,686	12,500	82,419	34,000	80,968	30,000	98,454	40,000	143,489
Black alone	15,067	6,000	51,480	0	4,760	0	20,875	16,500	57,449	32,000	105,822
Asian alone	3,940	18,000	102,264	2,000	35,462	70,000	132,051	125,650	170,887	105,000	238,511
Other (residual)	3,621	35,000	90,036	0	7,587	3,000	37,557	20,000	68,886	38,100	118,276
Hispanic origin (any race)	14,099	14,000	85,582	0	7,351	0	28,334	28,000	69,858	35,000	116,649
Not of Hispanic origin	104,590	15,490	86,903	3,000	43,280	35,000	79,583	30,300	96,687	41,000	144,016

Source: US Bureau of the Census.

CHAPTER 3

Establish a Budget

f your debt exceeds your income and assets, you should track your finances for at least a month to see where your money is spent. Commit yourself to tracking your expenses by keeping a copy of your receipts for everything you buy. To get a better handle on your cash, pay for everything with cash. Avoid using your ATM or bank card during that month, but if you must use your card, be sure to save all your receipts. It would be beneficial to track your expenses for three months, but by tracking for at least one month you will gain insight into how your income is spent.

At the end of the month that you track, add up your expenses. List your income and account for everything that counts as income, including child support and alimony. Deduct your monthly expenses from your net income. By net income, I mean your take-home pay and not your gross pay (pay before taxes and insurance). Once you have deducted your expenses from your net income, if the result is positive, it means that your income exceeds your expenses, which is great news! If, however, your expenses are greater than your income, you must cut down on your expenses and also cut down on debt.

I would go one step further and categorize your expenses by separating your fixed expenses from your variable expenses. Your fixed expenses are the expenses that you must pay at the end of the month and that you cannot get away from paying. Your rent, maintenance, or mortgage payment is a fixed expense, as is your car insurance, which you have to pay monthly, quarterly, or yearly. You may not have much wiggle room to reduce your fixed expenses.

To reduce your monthly expenses, you should look at your variable expenses, which may include your weekly grocery bill and your dry-cleaning and entertainment and cable and travel bills, to name a few. These expenses vary and should offer more leeway in reducing expenses. If you normally buy filet mignon, perhaps try to avoid it altogether or at least buy less than you normally would. Your variable expenses hold the key to maneuvering. The money that you save from trimming these expenses can be used to reduce debt and increase your monthly savings. If you are in a position where expenses exceed income, or if you have a negative net worth, you should probably focus first on debt elimination or reduction. Ultimately, the money you spend reducing debt is money saved from having to pay high-interest rates or fees.

Once you have eliminated or greatly decreased your debt, you are in an I.D.E.A.L. position to accumulate savings and investments. Your I.D.E.A.L. strategy is to pay yourself first! Just like you had an obligation to first pay monthly debt, the focus should now be on your savings and investments. By paying yourself first, you will be well on your way to accumulating financial wealth. To facilitate paying yourself first, you should set up an automatic savings plan through which your bank automatically deducts from your paycheck the amount you designate and deposits the funds directly into your savings or investment account.

Commit yourself to automatically save or invest. Once you do, you will be in a much better financial position and will be able to more quickly achieve your financial plan.

Table 2. Income and Expense Statement		
Monthly Income	_____	
Less: Monthly Expenses		
Savings	_____	(Pay yourself first.)
Investments	_____	
Rent or mortgage	_____	
Telephone	_____	
Electricity	_____	
Gas or oil	_____	
Water/sewer	_____	
Food	_____	
Transportation	_____	
Loans	_____	
Insurance	_____	

Recreation	_____	
Child care	_____	
Health care	_____	
Property tax	_____	
Other	_____	

CHAPTER 4

Accumulate Wealth for Savings and Investments

No matter what anyone tells you about accumulating wealth, you must save and invest your money wisely. To do so, you must have a financial plan and be committed to that plan. Being committed means having to stick to the plan. Money saved in a savings account is considered safe since it is insured by the Federal Deposit Insurance Commission for up to $250,000 per account, but investment accounts like stocks, bonds, or mutual funds are considered risky and carry the potential for capital loss. Such invested funds are uninsured and the investment return tends to be higher as a result of your assumed risk of losing most, if not all, of your capital.

Savings accounts are considered low risk and tend to pay a lower interest rate. Such accounts include checking accounts, savings accounts, and certificates of deposit. Investment accounts include bonds, stocks, mutual funds, real estate, and commodities such as gold, silver, or diamonds.

Although funds invested in an investment account carry high risk in terms of capital-loss potential, they tend to keep up with inflation. To hedge against a complete capital loss, you should diversify your portfolio. By diversifying, investors protect their investments by allocating a portion of their investments in different investment vehicles so that they may have a percentage of their investments allocated to bonds, stocks, or index-traded funds.

Diversification is not completely free from the risk of loss of capital, but it does offer some protection in that you may not suffer from a total loss of capital if your portfolio is diversified.

Bear in mind that when you invest or buy the stocks, bonds, or shares of a corporation, you are in essence lending your hard-earned money to that institution, corporation, or government entity in the hope that the company will do well and you will be able to recoup your initial investment plus dividends or interest. The Rule of 72 tells you how long it will take for your investment to double. The formula is 72/interest rate = number of years it will take for your money to double. Alternatively, if you want to know the interest rate needed to earn double your money, the formula is as follows:

72/number of years = interest rate needed to double your money in the number of years selected

You need a financial plan or goal if you are serious about accumulating savings for investing. Your goal could be to reach financial security, buy a home of your own, buy a car, pay for your children's college education, open a business, or have a comfortable retirement. Whatever your goal, you need a financial plan to bring it to fruition. You can do it, and here is another I.D.E.A.L. strategy to help you on your way. All that is required is that you commit to the financial plan and believe that you can accumulate wealth for yourself and your family.

To be financially secure, as with everything in life, you must have a plan, a road map, if you want to get there. You must have a plan to adhere to your goal of financial freedom and to break the chains of financial enslavement. Your plan must incorporate a way to reduce or eliminate debt, as has been outlined. Once your debt is paid off or has been greatly reduced, use the extra income to save and invest wisely.

Whether your financial plan is to save for a house, a comfortable retirement, a college education for yourself or for your children, or to create an emergency fund in case you become unemployed or underemployed, you have to first decide which goal you want to reach and how many years you have to achieve that goal. First, you need to find an investment plan that matches your time frame and invest accordingly.

You cannot blindly start a saving and investing plan without knowing where you stand financially. To do so, you should assess your current financial situation. You need to work on your personal financial statement, just like a business would, and set up your personal balance sheet. On a business balance sheet, the corporation lists its assets less its liabilities to find out how much equity the owner has in the business. You will need to do the same for your financial situation so that you know where you stand.

As mentioned, there are many types of savings accounts and retirement-savings accounts, such as 401(k), 403(b), IRAs, education-savings accounts, index-traded funds, and real-estate investment trust funds.

With a 401(k) retirement-savings plan, you may elect to have a percentage of your gross pay deducted from your paycheck every time you get paid, whether weekly, bi-weekly, semimonthly, monthly, or annually. Regardless of how often you get paid, the same percentage amount will be deducted from your pay.

The percentage amount that you elect to deduct will remain the same unless you decide to change it; however, the amount of money that gets deducted will vary depending on your gross pay for that period. If you work overtime or over a holiday or if your gross amount changes, the amount deducted from your pay will vary. The amount that gets deducted from pay is before taxes and insurance and other things are taken out.

The beauty of having the funds deducted for retirement savings is that the tax amount you pay decreases as a result. The reason is that once the percentage amount of retirement savings is deducted, you will be taxed on a smaller amount of gross pay. As a result, your net pay will be affected by the retirement-savings amount being deducted, but your net pay may not go down as much as the funds deducted for savings.

In other words, even though a large amount may be deducted from your pay to go toward your retirement-savings account, the difference in net pay will not decrease as much as the money that is being deducted.

Having an employer-sponsored retirement plan with a matching savings amount is one of the best ways to grow your retirement. The amount of retirement savings that is matched by your employer is responsible for your retirement-savings account growing much faster; before you know it, your retirement savings will have grown exponentially, making you more likely to accumulate long-term wealth.

Your retirement-savings account may be used to borrow against if you need to buy your primary residence and you are a first-time homebuyer, or you fund your or your child's college education, or you open a business. Check with your plan's administrators before submitting a request to borrow funds. They will tell you what is permissible. It is also wise to check with your accountant to determine the tax consequences of the withdrawal.

Be cautious when borrowing against your retirement-savings account because you will then have less money invested, which may cause you to receive a smaller return on your money.

If your company offers a matching retirement-savings plan, be sure to enroll as soon as you become eligible. No matter what you may need to sacrifice in order to enroll, invest at a minimum the percentage amount your company will match against your retirement-savings contribution. If you do not invest at a minimum the corporate-matching percentage amount, you will leave free money on the table every time you get paid—money that could be used to fund your retirement-savings plan.

Table 3. How Interest Compounds at Different Interest Rates & Investment Amounts

Initial Investment	Interest Rate	Year One	Year Two	Year Three	Year Four	Year Five
$ 1,000.00	5%	$ 1,050.00	$ 1,102.50	$ 1,157.63	$ 1,215.51	$ 1,276.28
1,000.00	6%	1,060.00	1,123.60	1,191.02	1,262.48	1,338.23
2,000.00	5%	2,100.00	2,205.00	2,315.25	2,431.01	2,552.56
2,000.00	6%	2,120.00	2,247.20	2,382.03	2,524.95	2,676.45
5,000.00	5%	5,250.00	5,512.50	5,788.13	6,077.53	6,381.41
5,000.00	6%	5,300.00	5,618.00	5,955.08	6,312.38	6,691.13

The younger you are when you start investing in your retirement plan, the better off you may become due to the interest amount you will earn from compounding interest. Compounding interest is the interest that is earned on your earned-interest overtime. As a result, compounding interest helps your money grow faster over time, which is why it pays to invest early in life.

Table 4. How a $10,000 Investment Grows over Time — Assuming an 8% Interest Rate Compounded Annually

In Year	Amount	Year Old	Year Old	Year Old		
1	10,800.00	20	30	50		
10	21,589.25	30	40	60		
15	31,721.69	35	45	65		
20	46,609.57	40	50	70		
25	68,484.75	45	55	75		
30	100,626.57	50	60	80		
35	147,853.44	55	65	85		
40	217,245.21	60	70	90		

The moment I became eligible to enroll in my employer's retirement-savings plan, I did so. I always elected to invest at least the maximum amount my employer was matching, which allowed my retirement savings to grow dramatically over a number of years. Close to ten years later, and as part of my master's degree in diplomacy, I elected to do an internship. I was fortunate to be selected to intern at the US Department of Commerce. My employer at the time was going through remediation and flat-out refused short-term leave that would allow me to fulfill this degree requirement. As an immigrant, I knew the internship would also help me give back to my adoptive country that has been so good to me.

So while I was on mandatory vacation leave from my job, I decided to head to Washington, DC, to start the internship and perhaps find a chance to explain why I may not be able to complete the internship after all.

In the middle of my mandatory two weeks' vacation, my employer wrote to me at home to say that if I didn't return to work at a certain time, I would be considered as having resigned. This was an investment bank for which I started, along with my supervisor, the custody department.

To say that I spent a number of years working late every night and on weekends is an understatement. Never once did I complain because I loved my job, and no sacrifice was too great for me to make. In certain instances, those sacrifices were to the detriment of my family life.

After receiving that letter, I decided to stay and complete my internship. I felt betrayed by the company to which I had given so much of my time and some of the best years of my working life.

The decision to stay and complete the internship was the best decision for me because soon afterward almost everyone was offered a package in one of the departments of the bank. I tell you my personal story to make the point that if it had not been for the contributions I made while employed at the company in question, I would have been in financial trouble.

I love business and have always had an entrepreneurial mind-set, so my best friend and I decided to form an LLC to invest in real estate. I also consider real estate one of the vehicles to create or accumulate wealth, and knowing that I wanted to eventually invest in such an endeavor, I took it upon myself to learn as much as I could about investing in real estate. Eventually we did purchase our first investment property. It is a two-unit apartment; one is currently rented and pays the expenses for itself, while the second is renovated and just came on the market as a rental, which will generate passive income for me and my business partner.

I share this information to offer an example of how far my retirement savings have taken me. I have gone from being unemployed as the proud holder of two master's degrees to becoming the cofounder of an LLC and a real-estate investor.

I am glad to have had the opportunity to invest in a retirement-savings plan because the money invested helped sustain my real-estate investing dream. Yes, there were tax consequences for using my retirement-savings plan to invest in real estate, and there were also risks inherent in the deal, but if I had to do it over the only thing I would do differently is contribute more to my retirement-savings plan.

Not everyone is fortunate enough to have a company-sponsored retirement plan; to have one with a matching savings plan is now rare, but a plan without matching is no longer an impediment to investing thanks to President Obama's executive order, myRA.

Most people undoubtedly know that saving for retirement is the first step toward securing a solid retirement. With that in mind, myRA was created so that if you want to start saving for retirement, you can do so through a myRA account. In his January 28, 2014, State of the Union address, President Obama directed the US Department of the Treasury to create myRA, a retirement-savings account that acts as a stepping stone for anyone wishing to prepare for retirement who does not have access to an employer-sponsored retirement plan, such as a 401(k).

Almost anyone with an income under $191,000 a year is eligible to open a myRA savings account. Workers who sign up for a myRA savings account through their employer are eligible to have a portion of their paycheck, up to an annual maximum of $15,000, directly deposited into their myRA savings account.

You do not need a lot of money to invest in a myRA account, nor do you need to contribute a large amount of money to maintain your account. Contributions to a myRA can be as low as five dollars per pay period through payroll deductions. Upon separation from your employer, you have the option to roll over your myRA into a private-sector retirement account.

There are many benefits associated with having a myRA retirement-savings account. One advantage is that the money invested is secure and any contributions made will never decrease in value. Funds invested are backed by the government and contributions can be withdrawn tax-free any time (Secretary 2014, 1).

As with any investment you intend to make after reading this book, please check with your accountant and financial advisor before you do so. Everything in life includes an element of risk, so be sure to learn as much as you can before you invest. There are horror stories of people losing their hard-earned money by making the wrong investments. Be certain that you are not one of these people by doing your homework every time you invest!

To arrive at your net worth, you should list on a piece of paper all your assets, such as the value of your home, your savings-account balance, your retirement-plan amount, the value of your jewelry, and so on. Almost anything that you own that has a monetary value when sold is an asset, such as your car. Once you have listed all your assets, list your liabilities, which is what you owe on your debt to your creditors.

Once you have your liabilities or debts listed, such as the balance on your mortgage, your student loans, your credit-card debt, or anything that you owe to a creditor, list every debt—no matter how small. Take the total of your calculated assets and deduct your total liabilities or debt. If the result is positive, my congratulations because this means that your assets exceed your liabilities and you have a positive net worth.

Conversely, if you display a negative balance, this means that your debts are greater than your assets and you have a negative net worth. You need major intervention to get you on the road to financial freedom, but do not despair or become discouraged because you can do it! If I can, anyone else can too. It will be hard work and will require sacrifice on your part, but at the end of the day you will be in a better financial position. The sacrifices you make now will be well worth it in the long run.

With a negative net worth, you need to follow the outlined plan to get out of debt or at least minimize your debt. There is no getting around the debt issue if you are serious about breaking the chains of financial enslavement.

Table 5. Net Worth Statement				
Assets	**Current Value**	**Liabilities**	**Amount**	**Difference**
Cash	_____	Mortgage balance	_____	n/a
Checking account(s)	_____	Credit card(s)	_____	n/a
Savings	_____	Personal loan(s)	_____	n/a
Life insurance— cash value	_____	Car loan(s)	_____	n/a
Retirement account(s)	_____	Student loan(s)	_____	n/a
Real estate	_____	Other	_____	n/a
Other investments	_____		_____	n/a
Personal property	_____		_____	n/a
Total	_____	**Total**	_____	_____

CHAPTER 5

Live below Your Means

One of the keys to continued financial success is to live below your means once you achieve your definition of financial freedom. Recognize when you have reached your financial goal and give thanks to any higher power you believe in and to the people who supported you while you were on your journey of financial discovery.

After reaching their goals, some people will tend to spend more because more money is available. Your goal should not be to spend uncontrollably and squander your newfound wealth; instead, you should value your wealth. Unless you happen to have been born wealthy or married and inherited wealth, your financial achievement probably took you some time to attain. Treat your wealth with respect and do not shop uncontrollably. More specifically, do not accumulate new debts. If you purchase something on credit, pay it off before you accrue penalties and interest. Whatever you do, do not fall victim to debt!

The ease with which people fall victim to debt is why it is important to live below your means. I know it might sound easier said than done, but as the saying goes, "Where there is a will, there is a way." Learn to separate the things that you actually need to survive from the things that you want. Often, we end up buying frivolously, so before you make a purchase, take a few minutes to think about what you are buying and whether it is a need or a want. If it falls under the "want" category, think about the reason you want to indulge in making the purchase.

To save money at the grocery store, buy things in bulk when they are on sale. Go on vacation during off-peak times to save what could possibly be hundreds of dollars.

If you are shopping for a car, why buy it new when you can buy it a few years older from a certified dealer and save thousands of dollars in the process? If you need to finance your car purchase, then you are not ready to buy the car, unless you are buying it to use as a business expense. In that case, by all means feel free to finance your purchase, but check with your accountant regarding the tax ramifications.

If you are buying a car for pleasure, it is best to pay with cash—whatever it is you can afford—so you can save thousands of dollars from not only the cash purchase, but from the savings you will gain by not having to pay finance and interest charges.

You may be tempted to buy a luxurious car when instead you can buy a less-expensive car and save big. Remember, the money you save and don't spend is the money you get to keep to enrich yourself and your family. The money you spend buying luxurious items is the money spent to enrich someone else. Opt to keep more money in your pocket, no matter how difficult that choice may seem.

CHAPTER 6

Advice from People Who Have Followed These I.D.E.A.L. Strategies on Their Own

Every person who has followed these I.D.E.A.L. strategies agrees that an education is the key to progressing in any aspect of life. By obtaining an education, they all believe that they experienced a better chance at succeeding in their career or profession. Parents who wish their children to be better off than themselves choose to sacrifice to give their children the right education.

One of the people I have interviewed attributes his success to the motivation he received from his parents. He stayed in school and remained disciplined and focused on his studies and eventually became an internationally known professional figure in his community. His path to success was through discipline, consistency in pursuing his goals, and hard work.

Another interviewee's path to success was to work as a home attendant while attending school. This interviewee eventually earned an associate's degree, got a job, went back to school to pursue a bachelor of science in nursing, earned a master's in public administration, and went back to school to become a nurse anesthesiologist, all while also investing in real estate. She accumulated several investment properties and paid them off and is now collecting rental income while she continues to work. She will soon retire with a good pension from the city in which she lives, along with her investment income from her personal retirement-savings account.

This person followed the path of school and real-estate investing and, along with her retirement investments, was able to achieve financial freedom. She kept her debts low by paying off often every credit-card bill before it was due to avoid paying finance charges or penalties. A friend of this particular person started on the same path by working as a home attendant, but due to family constraints and financial obligations had to take a different route.

She eventually went to school and became a certified nursing assistant and worked in health care, but never earned enough to be able to invest. Although this person recently retired, she still works at least two days a week to make ends meet. These two friends started out on the same level, but one chose to sacrifice everything to pursue a college education; the other tried but could not pursue higher education, although she was able to earn a certificate that allowed her to earn more than the minimum wage and helped her to live a financially decent life.

Another person I interviewed achieved success through education, hard work, and real estate. This particular person started school very late in life. Her mother immigrated to the United States when this person was very young. The family members that she grew up with did not send her to school, but as she grew a little older she moved in with her grandmother, who showered her with love and sent her to school beyond the age that most children attend.

She refused to let her age be a deterrent to her success in life. She excelled in school, her thirst for knowledge was so great. Upon coming to the United States, she went to junior high and eventually high school. She earned a scholarship to attend nursing school.

While in school, she worked and saved every penny. She used the money she earned, along with her scholarship money, to invest in real estate. She bought a condo near a college, where it would be in-demand. Upon graduation, she worked as a nurse and saved as much as she could. She eventually bought her own primary residence and used the equity in the house, which, along with her excellent credit, qualified her to get a mortgage to purchase a commercial property with at least two stores and several apartments.

This person is meticulous with her credit. She pays her bill on time every time and has near-perfect credit, which is a rarity today. Because of her real-estate investments and her astute business and finance acumen, she has grown her investments to save for her retirement and is free to travel any time she wants.

There are many additional examples I could offer, but I chose to share those that had the greatest impact on me. Because these are people I have personally known for a long time, I have witnessed them progress from one stage in their lives to the next. They started out as immigrants and became financially secure. They were not handed anything. They knew that if they wished to succeed, they had to work hard, watch their credit like a hawk, and save and invest for the future.

I could use as an example a person whose parents immigrated to the United States, though she was born in this country and raised in the suburbs in a middle-class family.

She went to an all-black private college and graduated with good grades. Eventually, she earned her master's and went on to teach. She had a good childhood and did not experience major childhood trauma, except for her parents getting divorced. She makes a very good income, upward of $120,000 as of the writing of this book, but she lives from paycheck to paycheck. She sends her children to private school, drives a car that is almost paid for, has student loans that are being repaid, and she has a mortgage and credit-card bills.

This person refuses to budget and spends her paycheck before she gets it. She is constantly borrowing against her retirement and finds it very difficult to make ends meet. She is a wonderful person but finds it difficult to control her credit, so she has to pay more to purchase items on credit and, as a result, is cash poor and trapped in a downward financial spiral.

I offer you these examples to help you find a formula that works for you and to help you evaluate your own financial story in relation to the examples these people provide. We may each take different paths to achieve financial success, but some things should be observed, such as safeguarding your good credit and not biting off more in debt than you can chew. Also, you should save your money and increase your level of investing.

Once you have achieved financial freedom, you should protect it in ways like buying insurance for property, health, disability, and your life. Health insurance protects your wealth against unexpected medical emergencies. Disability insurance protects your wealth by helping you pay your living expenses should you become disabled or injured for an extended period of time. You may be covered under your employer's disability-insurance benefits, but it makes sense to purchase personal disability insurance to supplement what you will receive from your employer's disability-insurance benefit plan. Life insurance protects your family by paying life proceeds to your beneficiaries. Homeowner's insurance protects you against, for example, loss from fire and theft. Depending on where you live, you may also need to buy flood insurance. Another option to help protect your wealth is to purchase long-term care insurance. It will prove helpful should you become ill and need to be placed in a nursing home. The younger you are when you purchase long-term care insurance, the less expensive your policy premiums will be.

This concludes the five I.D.E.A.L. strategies that I have outlined in this book. I hope you are able to learn a few things and that you will consider them as you blaze your own path to financial freedom. Please share this book with children in your family because children are never too young to learn financial skills. Try some with them—you may be amazed.

I'll use my four-year-old as an example: she has a chore in the house for which she earns five dollars a week. I don't force her to do it since she is quite young, but she is mature for her age. When she earns her five dollars for performing her chore, I have her write the amount in her financial book—yes, she writes it by herself. She writes how much she earns and whether or not she buys an ice cream or some other treat for herself; she has learned to deduct her expenses from the cash she has earned, so she knows that whatever is left is her savings to do with as she pleases. If she wants a new toy, she knows that she needs to save for it or go without if she does not wish to put all of her savings into one toy.

You can teach pretty much anyone money-management skills, but whether they wish to put these into practice is up to them. It was fun writing this book for young adults who are in high school and also for those who are about to enter college or have recently graduated. I hope you put these five I.D.E.A.L. strategies into practice so that by the time you are ready to retire, you will have enough money to retire on your own terms and avoid being a slave to your finances.

CHAPTER 7

Final Words of Advice

As you embark on the accumulation of wealth as outlined in this book, I would also like to provide you with some spiritual advice. As you go forward in life, remember that you have the most unique and fortunate opportunity, which is to be alive and able to write your own destiny.

You are uniquely positioned to be whomever you choose. Not even the sky is the limit of your potential. It is up to you to decide because you are not limited based on your social standing or your family background. Do not let anyone tell you otherwise. It is up to you to think about and determine how far you want to go in life; it is not dependent on what society imposes on you.

If you wish to reach for the sky or beyond, you only have to close your eyes and imagine your destination. Imagine what it is that you want to achieve and live your life knowing that you can accomplish whatever you wish during your lifetime. Imagine the power that you have in thinking new thoughts and ideas, and how you can bring them into fruition with some effort and determination. You will reach whatever goal you set for yourself, but don't put any limitations on yourself. You are free to think, to work, and to surmount anything that wants to stop you from achieving your full potential. Do not ever stop striving for bigger and better things. Step by step, you will find your way to your ultimate destiny in life.

Remember that the world is filled with poverty, and millions go hungry on a daily basis and suffer at the hands of people in search of money or "profit," as it is called in capitalism. Do empathize with these people as you go forth on your journey and imagine, if you can, a world where there is empathy in everyone's heart, one in which the few who have care for the many who do not have. There would be less suffering, but many people have yet to recognize that humankind's final resting place is not tied to money and is instead a place where nothing can be bought. Do not make the accumulation of money your sole reason for living; in the end, it is your deeds that will act as your spiritual currency. The more good deeds you perform, the more spiritual currency you will accumulate, and the easier your movement will be to a higher plane of existence—to a universal plane on which wants are things of the past. Call it paradise or nirvana, but it is your current good deeds that will propel you or your spirit to this higher plane of existence; earth is but a temporary stop in your ultimate evolution, and evolution is what makes the universe endure.

Everything evolves from one plane of existence to the next, and nothing is stagnant. Creativity is what keeps you alive, and humankind is meant to create because as we create, so we evolve. Evolution is meant for the fittest—the spiritually fittest, that is—in terms of our actions and our deeds. The more spiritual your soul is, the easier it is for you to move to a higher plane of existence, as life is perpetual, *ad infinitum*, and there is no end—we simply move up or down to different planes of existence. Life evolves and people evolve, so treat others how you wish to be treated.

As you go forward on your life's journey, remember that God is real; the Supreme Being or Supreme Power, as some people say, exists—not in the form you think or have been taught to believe, as the Supreme Being is creation itself. You can never imagine, even if you were to take a lifetime or multiple lifetimes to try. The essence of the Supreme Being exists in all of us, and anything that happens on this plane and beyond this time happens because God wills it! God wills only goodness for humankind, so live your life and put God first. You will have the power to achieve the impossible with faith, determination, and tenacity, so remember that everything you can see or imagine you can accomplish. Cultivate a do-good attitude and let love and light for every human being and object surround you in everything you do.

Use your God-given power of inspiration to create new products that will benefit humankind and create financial success for yourself in the process. You have the power that is inherent in every living soul, which is the power to create. As you create, you allow the entire world to evolve with your creation because creation is the seed of evolution, and every instance in existence involves creation and evolution. The more inspiration you gather around you, the more you can create, so remember that creation first exists in the unseen, in the abstract, and it takes just a single person to bring it into existence. That single person can be you! The seeds of creation have already been created and are at your disposal; all you need is to open your mind, be receptive, and tap into your God-given power of inspiration because you were made to create. With each passing thought, you put creation into motion, so imagine existence as a river in which everything lies motionless until one thought brings motion into creation, into life itself.

Keep yourself open and receptive, listening to God when he speaks to you. As you go about your daily life, do not let the fatigue of the mundane wear you out or stifle your creativity. Do you let anger or too much ambition and resentment stifle your creativity? Imagine the power of a mind at rest, free of negativity and able to think consciously and to create and evolve. Therein lies the power of creation because it must occur in a stable mind or environment that is free of stress, addiction, and negativity. Negativity, especially, will stifle your creativity, so relax your body and mind whenever you wish to tap into your power to create because it is a conscious decision, a decision that may alter your life in the process. Remember that you were created in the image of the Supreme Being and, as such, you embody the spirit and essence of the Supreme Being. Believe in yourself and in your power of creation because if you can think it in the unseen, you can bring it forth into the world. The world exists out of nothingness, or from a void of latent creation. Just because something is unseen does not negate the fact that it exists. The line between the visible and the invisible is created by the limitations we set upon ourselves; and once we remove the veil of limitations, our power to create is unlimited. Imagine the life you would live if you were not subject to the limitations you impose on yourself. With your creative process and abilities, the sky is not the limit for your potential. As it is in the unseen, so it is in the seen world. Everything that exists or will exist has already been created, and you only need vision, will, and determination to bring it forth into this plane of existence. As God said, "Let there be light!" Then and there, light came into being, but was light created out of thin air or was it already present in latent form and waiting to be manifested? Take this advice with you and live it, breathe it, and live it again and again: your power lies in your ability and capability to create. Creation brings evolution, and evolution transposes the entire human race's plane of existence to one that may yet be seen or be understood by all of humankind.

If you can put some of these things into practice, you may eventually lead a more fulfilling life and enjoy the fruits of your labor. Live a beautiful life filled with laughter, kindness, and empathy for others because the beauty of a life well lived is immeasurable. You only live once in a lifetime, so you only have one chance to get it right. A beautifully well-lived life carries no remorse, which is not to say that life should be a bed of roses, but it should be lived in such a way as to avoid regrets and imbalance and to have peace. So decide now whether your life will be a beautiful life lived with the intention of giving back to humanity as your brother's or sister's keeper.

A beautiful life is meant to be lived by giving back to humankind, to give of oneself as much as and as often as necessary because life on earth is a rare gift and we should live it! Live in the moment and say good-bye to the regrets of yesterday because today is a new day that brings with it the seeds of a new beginning. Every day is a new chance to start something and to hone the skills of your craft. How fortunate you are to be given a chance and the most beautiful and rarest gift of all: life!

The same new beginnings or new chances are given to everyone, regardless of social standing or economic background. Every day, we get the same chance to start something new, no matter our background or affiliation. Let regret and doubt dwell in yesterday and focus your thoughts and energy on today, where the seeds of a new beginning take hold in this amazing space we share and call the universe. New things, new beginnings, are burgeoning all around us, and we only need to look around us to see the beauty of life and be amazed! As you pursue financial success, take time to smell the roses and give back to humanity because being a conduit for goodness in the world is how you live a beautiful life filled with joy and happiness.

Conclusion

hope you have learned something from reading this book. If you have, I am happy to have shared my knowledge with you regarding how you can empower yourself financially. Financial freedom is not easy to achieve, but it is achievable. Many of us have faced roadblocks in our lives, whether in the form of the loss of a job, a family emergency, or an illness.

I hope this book reminds you that you are not alone. There are many people in the same situation. The difference between them and you lies in whether you choose to do something about your financial situation. This book is as much for me as it is for you. We are learning together how to make better financial decisions, how to get out debt, how to increase our credit score, and how to save more money. To be financially free takes a lot of hard work, commitment, and determination. Often you will be tempted to give up and not stay the course. I am advising you to forge ahead. Nothing good is ever easy. Every day, take a step toward achieving your goal. It could be as small as foregoing your regular cup of coffee from your favorite coffee shop. I advise you to make that small sacrifice. It will reinforce your determination to stay on track and stay motivated, knowing that each small step taken is an investment in your future financial freedom.

The most important strategy I would like for you to take from the book is that bad debt is enslaving your current and future cash flow. Bad debt is debt that you incur and that has a negative return to you. By negative return, I mean a debt you incur to buy an asset that does not increase in value—for example, buying a television on a credit card. A television is an asset that is not likely to increase in value over time, whereas a debt such as a mortgage on a house has the potential to increase in value over time. There may come a time when your property value may go down, but in the long run it should rebound. You have to live somewhere, so why not use the money that you would have used to pay rent to someone else to pay yourself rent instead? By doing so, you are embarking on the road to a more secure financial future.

It is always best to start investing at a young age in order to take advantage of compounding interest, which is interest earned on interest. Eventually, you want to stay away from bad debt, focus on reducing or eliminating debt, and save to invest, and you will earn your financial freedom. The strategies outlined in this book will work best if you follow the format to reduce debt, pay your bills on time, and be sure to call your creditors—do not wait for them to call you or send your debt to a collection company if you have trouble paying your bills. By calling first, you will show that you are conscientious and willing to pay your debt as soon as you are able. By talking to your creditors, they are more likely to understand your plight and be willing to work with you until your situation is resolved. Stay focused; don't lose sight of the decreased debt and increased savings and investments you envisioned.

I wish you great luck on your I.D.E.A.L. journey to financial freedom.

REFERENCES

Secretary, T. W. 2014. Fact Sheet: Opportunity for All: Securing a Dignified Retirement for All Americans.

www.ingramcontent.com/pod-product-compliance
Lightning Source LLC
Chambersburg PA
CBHW021445170526
45164CB00001B/406